Leah Larwood

Oneironaut

Indigo Dreams Publishing

First Edition: Oneironaut
First published in Great Britain in 2024 by:
Indigo Dreams Publishing
24, Forest Houses
Cookworthy Moor
Halwill
Beaworthy
Devon
EX21 5UU

www.indigodreamspublishing.com

ISBN 978-1-912876-88-4

British Library Cataloguing in Publication Data. A CIP record for this book can be obtained from the British Library.

Designed and typeset in Palatino Linotype by Indigo Dreams.
Cover illustration *The Wisdom Within* by © Lucy Campbell
Front cover layout by Kirsty Tizzard
Printed and bound in Great Britain by 4edge Ltd.

Papers used by Indigo Dreams are recyclable products made from wood grown in sustainable forests following the guidance of the Forest Stewardship Council.

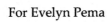

For Evelyn Pema

Acknowledgements

Firstly, I'd like to express my gratitude to Dawn and Ronnie for their support and belief. With my thanks also to the following who have awarded prizes, commended or placed some of the poems in this collection: Poetry News Members' Competition 2016; Poetry Society's Stanza Competition 2018; Poetry Book Society Mslexia Competition 2019; Magma Poetry Competition 2022; Candlestick Press 2023; Troubadour International Poetry Prize 2024. Thank you also to the magazines, journals, anthologies and broadcasters for publishing or airing poems including: Aesthetica Creative Writing Award 2024 Anthology; Alchemy Spoon; BBC East; BBC Three Counties; Indelible Literary and Arts Journal; Ink, Sweat & Tears and New Welsh Review. Special thanks to early mentors Helen Ivory and Sean O'Brien, and later, for the invaluable manuscript support from Liz Berry and Mimi Khalvati. Many thanks to my friend and often first reader Jenny Pagdin. Thanks to other generous readers: Vanessa Lampert, Judith Fitzsimons, Julia Webb and the Norwich Stanza.

Thanks to the Samye Ling sangha and the late Chöje Akong Tulku Rinpoche, without whom this collection wouldn't exist. A special mention to Charlie Morley, one of the best lucid dreaming guides any oneironaut could wish for, and who has inspired many poems including *An Ode to Nightmares*. Witchy thanks to the unsurpassable 'Coven' (special 'Boom!' to Judith, for your care during those bleary-eyed days). I-Thou thanks to Tim, Liz, fellow SCPTI peers and ATMs, past and present – and to Simon. Poetry therapy thanks to Dr. Geri Chavis and Victoria Field. My gratitude to Dan, Laura G, Steve, Skippy, Laura M, Emma and Cathy for your support. A heartfelt thanks to Mum, my rock, for everything. To Dad for his zest in dream work and storytelling, and Matthew for his loyal support and cheerleading at every reading. Above all, my deepest thanks to my daughter Evelyn Pema (and Peanut & Pistachio the quokkas).

Lastly, thank you to you all, for reading this collection.

CONTENTS

Author's Note

In 1918, after experiencing the atrocities of the trenches, my paternal grandad Bramwell Reginald Larwood returned from WW1 aged eighteen. Chap, as he was known, was an electrical engineer, and avid piano player in Norwich pubs. Although he served in, and survived both world wars, he lived the rest of his life experiencing unspeakable flashbacks and nightmares. If only they knew then what they now know about PTSD.

In contrast but perhaps not coincidental, since I was a teenager, my favourite nocturnal pursuit became lucid dreaming – a subject that has become increasingly mainstream over the last decade. The term lucid dreaming was first coined in 1913 by writer and psychiatrist, Frederik van Eeden. It's a type of dream in which you know that you are dreaming and are able to exert some influence over the dream – sometimes to support psychological or spiritual growth, other times just for fun. Included as a practise within 'dream yoga' by Tibetan Buddhists, lucid dreaming has been part of a wide range of cultures and religions for centuries. Yet the scientific community only started to recognise it after research from Harvard and Stanford Universities in the 1970s. Since then, some studies have shown it can reduce symptoms of anxiety and cure PTSD.

Other sleep states you will see referenced in this collection include the hypnogogic, the state we pass through *before* we fall asleep. Then there's the hypnopompic, a broad, pure and refined state we experience shortly *after* we surface from sleep.

Over the last decade, these poems kept surfacing from my sleep and (lucid) dreams and this is where they have landed.

I dedicate the spirit of these poems to my grandad Reg whom I never met, and to anyone else afraid of the night – for it's sometimes in these frightening realms where the gold can be found.

Impermanence

Like stars, mists and candleflames,
Mirages, dew-drops and water-bubbles
Like dreams, lightning and clouds,
In that way I will view all composite phenomena.

*~ Wishing Prayer
from the Kagyu Tibetan Buddhist lineage ~*

Oneironaut is Leah Larwood's debut collection, and joint winner of the Indigo First Poetry Competition 2023.

Oneironaut

Oneironaut *Noun. oneironaut (pl. oneironauts).*
An explorer of dream worlds, usually associated with lucid
dreaming. A person who has the ability to travel within a
dream on a conscious basis. Such a traveller in a dream may be
called an oneironaut. *Pronounced: Oh-nigh-ronaut.*

Oneironaut

Please RSVP by dream

Meet me at a safe place
by the sea, where the lemon sharks
swim under bougainvillea stars.
Place your night eyes in and drop
low. Stay awake as you drift –
join me when you can.

For now, there's a darker storm
where time-travelling beams
hoodwink the night;
where caged shadows emerge
and the vanishings leave you
with a belly full of rocks.

Together, we may reach the unknown
and when the mountains close in?
We don't have much time.
Dreamers, for when I can't get back,
meet me inside a dream.
Look for a mandala in tarnished brass.

Will you let me in? Just in case
I can't get back. Send word at midnight
through space, time and sea.
For now, all that was
seems brighter, and past the dead
palms I can feel a welcome

across the border. I'm long-vanished
but scarlet wings are rising
from the falling embers.

Hypnogogic Sleep at the Hairdressers

I like stealing hairgrips
from your apron pocket,
that dangerous space
between your groin and hip
presses lax against my arm.
Shaped in your palms,
my bouncing layers
swing to the swish
of your scissor snip,
my eyelids hang low
and the buzz of
salon white noise
sends me back in utero.
Now there's a juju
behind my eyes, gold
saliva from a candle light
that jolts, and I drift
to the beach of tears.
Resting in the underbelly
of sleep – I sail
to an empty place
wide awake, out
at sea, until your hand
tests my shoulder,
a trashy magazine falls.
You smooth out
my poker-straight
rescued mane.
I'm truckled pink.
You take back
the hair grip.

From Under the Wardrobe

the naked bulb on the ceiling
is an oddly lit glass balloon,

bobbing riskily upside down
in the winter sky.

There's an unfriendly quality
in my shoulder;

I'm packed like a fugitive's
suitcase, roughly. Buried

under hanged clothes
that belong to me. When I fell,

I saw flickering street lights
and his slurred yawn.

The winged doors flapped
open, fixed around me

like a mother's jaws. I lie
awake inside my casket,

counting each crushed breath,
waiting for kinder voices

to reach me. The only thing
I recognise is the white tilted sky.

Jackdaw
After Charles Bukowski's Bluebird

there's a jackdaw in my head
she's in charge of dark matter

calls the shots from the back room
light bulb swinging above her desk

I hear her typing late at night
the quiet genius that stays behind.

now and then she pokes her beak
through the trapdoor of my day

while I fidget, sip weak coffee
she listens to stories in the room

collects novel faces, tiny voices
chatters voicemails in my dreams.

when we meet a friendly stranger
and I'm tangled or feeling coy

I toss her the attic key and say
sure, let's see what you've got.

now she wants to stay out and
I'm like, what now jitterbug?

they can't see too much of you
but after a pisco sour too many

she slinks out the small door
of my mouth. she's not so sly.

as we glide into bed that night
I watch her skinny belly rise

softly stroke her flaky beak
slur, *shhh* it's alright, stay close

you can keep that key, for now.

What Lies Below Sleep

Will you find yourself awake inside your dreams?
What will you do: watch the worm moon half-undress,

relive your fondest memories? You could always
"sleepwalk through life" or else find other comfort

kipping in the yew trees or watching the dead cities
somersault. Now and then be a curious waterfowl,

always take a deep lungful and wear webbed feet
to peek underneath and reach the bulk of the iceberg.

Below the water line you can see every fallen hope and
hidden love, every voiceless wish; an aquarium of grief.

You might find your connection with spirit and universe
down there or perhaps you'll be a tourist, fly under water

and bungee jump till dawn. As you stir, slow-dance
with fragmented beams, deep in the duvet of waking.

Failing that, you might just see what it feels like to be
limbless and unbound, wide awake in low-hung sleep.

Nocturnal Gifts

Dreams are stocking fillers untied
with heart strings upon waking.

Prophetic dreams are the crystal
balls behind your eyelids.

A lucid dream is a champagne flight
to Saturn in a hot air balloon.

A golden shadow dream is a tiara
made of untouchable metallic awe.

Nightmares are well-meaning
letters regretfully left unopened.

Lucid nightmares are pocketfuls
of coal spun into Hope Diamonds.

A dreamless sleep is full of dusty
parcels, waiting for you to notice.

Six Lucid Dream Entries

It began in summer at her loneliest.
Three men sang to her by comet-light,
as they tumbled together in fresh laundry.
She was woken by her mother
dragging her legs off the end of the bed.

In India, she didn't talk for nine days
and ten nights, lived off sweet lentils,
red rice. At dawn, she asked the dream
to show her something important –
she saw the face of her unborn child.

Three midwinters later she was frozen
in a claustrophobic house. Night after night
she would dive in a sea of turquoise oil
above the lemon sharks, as she swam
with hand-drawn starfish in her hair.

In Regent's Park, a beautiful Indian man
with sapphire eyes danced with her.
I am your psyche, your ex-husband.
He took her hand, drew a heart in her palm
with the end of his listless tongue.

Four months after giving birth, tethered
to bricks, mortar and the brink of madness,
she rode her bicycle down St Clements' Hill,
the wind in her blouse, her wicker basket
filled with the freedom of time and eggs.

Trees That Trigger Lucid Dreams

Don't think the garden loses its ecstasy in winter.
It's quiet. But the roots are down there riotous ~ Rumi

One luminous dawn before the winter solstice,
when morning couldn't shake off night
and the afternoon mantled a shadowy cloak,

that's when the December trees first spoke to her.
She'd long forgotten the fullness of July maples
with their glib sway and vacant, plump swag.

Yet as her exhales travelled to the ceiling of night,
there was movement in the wild thicket.
She rose into the upright sunlight of her dream

with the moon peeking over its thorny shoulder,
skeleton branches clawing at her bedroom window.
The sound rooted her between awake and slumber.

There, she held space between the borders of sleep.
Upon waking she started to walk through walls
and forgot how to hide or to bury or to look away.

Five Sleep Potions for Troubled Nights

I ~ *Moon Daisy (Ox-eye): For Night Coughs*

While the world loses its mind in reverie, this *fleur de la nuit*
revels in moonlight, casting shadowy hopes with its long stem,
large extrovert face beaming up at the moon. Unlike its sibling,
the garden daisy, the Ox-eye daisy never sleeps. Use leaves
in salads or steep flowers to make a ribcage-soothing tea.

II ~ *Poppy: The Insomniac Plant*

Take a teaspoon of tincture before bed to aid sleep. Remember,
harvest the common red *Papaver Rhoeas*, not the opiate variety,
Papaver Somniferum, which can cause slurred speech, confusion,
memory loss, pupil constriction, dilation and possible death.
Soak the petals in vodka and sip in between the sheets of unrest.

III ~ *Mugwort: The Lucid Plant*

For calming the nerves or as a way to lucid dream, this herb will also
relieve the soreness of feet. Found in waste lands and hedgerows,
Mugwort is a mild psychoactive also taken for hallucinogenic effect.
Dried leaves make a bedtime tea. While lucid, explore the basement
of your dream and befriend your shadow, mood-dependent.

IV ~ *Hemlock: The Big Sleep*

Best consumed in a salad or soup – but only if you wish to dive
deep beyond dream, and wake inside another. Hemlock grows
in small erect umbrella clusters. Flowers develop into a green, deeply
ridged fruit. Part of the carrot family and Socrates' choice of poison:
leading to asphyxia and a fixed, sardonic grin upon death.

V ~ St John's Wort: Fear of the Dark

To soothe nightmares, bad dreams or fear of the night, make a St. John's Wort Pillow. Fill a small cloth bag or old pillowcase with flower tops, fear, and any undesirables you have to hand. Stitch or tie the open end firmly shut. With a small knife, make an incision and gently place the bag under your skin.

Hypnos' Twin

Half of every human life
belongs to Hypnos.

During the psychosis
of blinding night,

red poppy in hand
like a night light,

your dreams
offer you the Earth.

When it's time
to meet his twin

and you notice
your final moon

you understand
your dreams

have just been a
death rehearsal.

According to Greek mythology, Hypnos (god of sleep) lived next to his
twin brother, Thanatos (personification of death), in the Underworld,
where light never reaches them.

Dreaming as Psychosis

Last night we became flagrantly
psychotic. It'll happen again tonight.
As before every single night
without fail, we hallucinate;

believe things that could not,
should not, be true. The clock
becomes an eye in the wall
and your hand, unhaunted,

reopens a familiar story.
Watching loved ones turn into
figurines. Feeling certainty
and fear at the same time.

Yet morning comes, we don't
seek psychiatric advice, we don't
tell a soul. We pour out our day
and get on with the coffee.

The Zoo in My Cellar

There's a GoPro
rigged up to the zoo
in my cellar, a direct line
to the editing suite, once the
lights pop out, the night vision
kicks in and chimpanzees break
into the Cognac. Baby owls start
swearing, pumas zig-zag across the
stairs, a flamingo makes eyes at a mop
vultures pick over regrettable conversations
and a tiger thwacks several shades of rage into
a feature cushion. Meanwhile, the snapping turtles
play ankle bingo and two Luna moths fly a figure of
eight over two quokkas discussing a new Netflix series.
A melancholic gorilla's writing in his diary. An edgy camel
searches for some herb. Lion's having a profound moment of
awareness about his friends, while zebra violins Dizzee Rascal's
You've Got The Dirtee Love. The hippos roll their eyes at the pandas,
the pandas roll them back across the floor. Dear old polar bear? He's
saying a prayer. Yet only the meditating bat knows that this can't go on
forever. Watching everything there's a capybara, still as sunrise, holding
a flute like a spell.

Dirty Laundry

White as moon bone and piled up lavishly,
exhausted limb, upon limb, upon
member, above midnight
severed sheets.

Ceiling-pegged pigtails in scarlet bows
hang for a noose, and the crows they
are a jumping foot to foot
to a rotten hymn.

At the top, stacked eyeballs in plum jars,
the icing of our laundry, and the sun
is our egg, shinning onwards
like the great forgetting.

Underneath it all, there's something
parched and tussling and pure
like a bud before the frost,
gasping for words.

*In a lucid dream I had during 2019, Helen Ivory (who represents an inner
poetry mentor) encouraged me to write a poem about 'the heap'.*

House Without Walls

In the dead of morning mother is missing.
A tornado has spat the house out whole
and the walls have fallen back into the night.

The one room still whole is the kitchen
illuminated by a blanket of dandelion light
that bounces off the tiles onto every clean spot.

The ceiling fan is spinning to a standstill.
I orbit each gutted living space, searching for her
- all that is left is infinity in the place of windows.

I sink into the uprising voice from below
where pipes have burst as if purgatory is leaking,
and speaking in her mother tongue to the floor -

my grandmother in blinkers mops puddle craters,
drips land in echo. As I edge into dampness,
catch my breath past the butchery blackness,

I hunt every desperate wall-less room for her
but my breaking bones tell me she's already gone.
Around the last corner I find a suspended stage

with upturned microphones and instruments
and four slaughtered band members; the music
has only just stopped, *the show is over.*

In the middle of the basement there's a wall
with the answer: an illegible name in sticky red
and she's there, the only audience member,

head back, laid to dry in the midday Maltese sun,
she's lost 40 years, gained obsidian hair, and eyes,
including the one she lost to a firework as a child.

I rest my lips on hers and then the dream begins
or else the ghost of it lays wet fingers on my neck
while my breath keeps us staring into the underworld.

Antechamber

On her breast rests the shadow of death's face.
She's felt it only once before, it's gentle regard
pressed on her brow like the shade of a thorn.

When the jasmine blossom was at its loveliest
it told her she will die in a spartan wilderness
in the warm summer darkness before the rain.

After hungry faces fade into endless walls
and the sky turns the colour of a fresh bruise.
How and when she leaves will tell us nothing.

She knows what lies behind, and what lies before
does not matter, for now she wakes in her sleep
her body reaches past, casting shadows in bloom.

Midnight Feast

Just after midnight she turns up
unannounced, hands me
a tangled daisy chain, asks for
Turkish Delight, and a peg
to hang fury and shame on.

Together, we open her emerald
satchel, examine its fullness
in silence. There are several things
she wants to unpack, so we tip
the whole mess on the carpet.

Her eyes drop like a question
that has patiently waited.
She looks up to the sky and
watches the crow-shaped clouds,
then hands me an item to examine.

Here, take this bow for your hair.
I cherished that long lilac ribbon,
my mother bought one sunny
December. Now mother is dead,
I feel desperately lost.

So I hand the child some hot
chocolate in an heirloom mug.
We sit shoulder to crown and watch
the day rise as our nightmares
cross-stich over breakfast.

The Sleep Thief

a toddler-sized burglar
with a balaclava and an innocent
waddle breaks into his mother's room
with an empty backpack
and pinches the smooth skin
from under her eyes

he places the silk in his back pocket
and reaching into her treasure trove,
takes conversations she once had
with friends, impulsive and searching sex
the sighs of indolent lunches
a peaceful cup of tea, a private wee

he unzips a side pouch and in that places
a longed-for trip to New Zealand
an afternoon of Katharine Hepburn fireside
he takes all her duvet days
and in her bottom drawer deposits
one thousand lunar phases

he surveys the room
with his foot idly crushes a Wotsit
into her Persian rug
then jumps into her bed –
something tumbles from his hoodie –
it lands on her lips, a lotus-scented kiss

the most precious she will ever know
and in the first moment of day-raw
searching for the stolen covers
she wakes ransacked yet overflowing
her wrist a crowbar
hooked around her sleeping loot.

A Cure for Insomnia

I have never seen poppies
like the ones I ran through
in that Norfolk field
a silent sea of scarlet
and a four-year old hand
clutching forgetfulness
and mislaid sleep
a reminder of loss
and renewal. Now
just a photograph
beyond wastelands
with stems of blood lush
petals, gossamer fine
that drop from the touch
of a different little finger
one twisted around
my night. Between cries
I sip its tincture
a soothing sedative
of dream and sleep.
Weed of summer,
I am floral drunk.

Oneironaut

Her first time felt like the closed mouth of purgatory;
she wondered whether this was what it was like
to be dead, to be awake when asleep,
yet she felt the most alive she had ever been.

Her first time felt like a summer's day in midwinter:
she could feel the sea spray on her dry tongue,
plum sky on her crown, sun seeping
into her gelid lungs like liquid caramel.

Her first time was like finally meeting
the caged bird in her head. Morning had broken
and jackdaw had spoken, black as guilt,
jabbering at her from the inside.

Her first time was brief. Two minutes
by her calculation yet the accountancy of sleep
told her, from her toppling viewing tower,
it could have been an hour or a lifetime.

Her first time felt like living inside a poem.
Each moment hung in front of her eyes.
Yet as she rode the sea on her back
everything spilled over into forgetfulness.

An Ode to Nightmares

Oh Nightmares, who would have dreamt
that all along you were the teachers
of life's sleepwalkers, a door to enlightenment.
Yet you remain unsung heroes:
tellers of truth, blacksmiths of dream.
You are the best-kept secrets of sleep;
only you expose the brilliance held under terror.

Sweet Dreams, your slick, faultless cousins,
take all the glory. Day Dreams too,
but next to you they're nothing but fanciful delusions,
dare I say, whimsical. Without your wild wisdom
the entire world wouldn't hear the alarm bells echoing.
Nightmares, you've been underestimated, only
you have the power to transform phobias of the night.

Without you, how would we know
which inner conflicts to attend to? We understand,
you roar for the greater good. Your message
is more urgent that your average pipedream.
You might be more rambunctious than dreams
about being naked in public or teeth falling out –
but you're not tyrants, you just want to be heard.

You may need to work on your reputation a little.
Nothing a PR campaign wouldn't sort.
A suitable slogan: *Nightmares,*
Lively Yet Well-Meaning Dreams! #StayWoke.
Then, one day, when folks ask one another:
How did you sleep? *Well,* they'll reply,
I had a dazzling nightmare.

Alchemy of Sleep

When night turns to ice and where
walls turn to rain turn to sea, after
half-light turns to day dark and where

beds turn to urns and time turns to you
and sky turns to dust. Where door opens
to field and wild fear turns to white gold.

Come morning, train times unravel
hairlines yet the day still snores and
you bear the cold war of your dream.

Lucid Dream Catcher

While the midnight of my dreams find breath
her cot a storm and our sleep too brief,

I feel warmth towards the lotus of death,
like the bright side of the moon's tender grief.

There are no words for the sorrow she streams.
Many long nights spent pacing for grace.

Where do they hide, those unborn dreams,
resting in waiting rooms, writhing in space?

Though I love her yawns to the scarlet skies,
we stay boxed in dusk-bolted night.

Finally we sleep. When I unwrap my eyes,
I'll give in to wonder, lean into the bright.

Sleep When the Baby Sleeps

I'd buy Ethiopian coffee from Norwich Market,
January tulips. The fishmonger would sell me
a fist of fish the size of your hand. A bundle
of beetroot, earthy planets hanging from a tote.

I'd inhale the warmth of passing sentences,
almond croissants. Almost home, a bundled
papoose bobbing to my walk, my steps racing,
you'd drift slowly to the sound of my hopes.

I'd release the sling carefully onto my bed,
tip-toe you down inside a plump barricade
of pillows. Lie beside you like a feather and
when I finally found the folds of hypnogogic,

you'd wake the dead. I'd fall into a wild mixture
of exhaustion and loss unable to rescue me
from you, or you from the silent grief broadcast
into our invisible chord. On better days we'd nap,

while YouTube lullabies seeped into the fabric
of our dreams. Youth leaking from my crown
like a fountain of untempered gold. Yet I'd always
yearn to be that arm of light reaching off into the hall.

Night Rainbow

I wait here
by the gold pot
end of hope,

counting beams
full and wide.
  Tonight

the moon
holds a mirror
to the rain,

colour soars,
and a Nightjar
churrs encore.

Starstruck,
I cheer the air
in somersault.

I'm not very sad,
I understand –
magic can return.

Gold Divers
For Judith

Your heart and my heart are very,
very old friends ~ Hafez

Cadence had a tendency to lie down
in the middle of the road to think.

It was the one place she found Hope –
the one other mother that felt like her.

Each mother was chin-deep in childhoods:
their own, their child's, that webbed space between.

Speaking in tongues, the women occasionally levitated
every time they had a certain kind of dream.

They both awoke at the same time.
A hand in each other's pocket, they walked for eons.

Everything can be illuminated by water,
or most things.

At day raw, in the unkempt darkness
the two women knelt by the lake and

submerged their entire heads and shoulders;
the lakebed spoke back to them.

What sung to them were their whole beings
like autumn's dusky melancholy.

Everything they didn't know they wanted
was there, buried weather under water.

They turned to each other, eyes like Neptune
and kissed. Each diving deeper,

they pulled out their six year old selves and
sacks of hidden treasures covered in algae.

They emerged steadfast and dizzy,
two entirely whole beings, at large.

On their way back to their husbands,
they walked straight into a place

with broad grins, pink gin, silence
and the strange narrow vision of it all.

It wasn't even a bar, more of a broom cupboard
pressed up against blue velvet wallpaper.

They opened their sacks onto the table
and everything spilled out.

Shadow Work as Thunder

Those invisible hands held up
in sky could not wait to clap,
even the sunset
stood out of earshot
as it stole the show
that night: it was like
nothing I'd ever dreamed of –
one hour long as day,
taking only short breaks
for outfit changes,
a diva in flashing black,
goddess in strapless moonbeams –
a boundless energy, bottled up
for too long. All the while,
I keep one eye on the weather.
I read the papers,
practise cross-stich,
recite mantras,
I've tried it all. This
was one thunderstorm I survived.
Unlike that other one, the day
I grasped my knees,
peeled away asphalt
with my tongue,
reached below the soil table
for a colour close to
midnight rose. Back on earth
the belting above
keeps me alive.
That's what I dream
for my child –
to run into the storms,
heart fastened on with frenzy,
hands held up in sky.

Preparation for Retrograde

Under a silver coloured sky
I tuck a blade in the folds of my dress,

wait for another orbit before I follow.
For a split in time, Neptune is static,

showers of star dust spitting out light.
Small particles open rivers in the sky

everything moves in reverse –
and a box flips open.

A wise woman hands me a crimson
coloured bar, sweet like quince jelly.

I swallow it whole and wake
knowing everything could happen.

What happened next in the dream (I)

I'm alone on a circle of sunlit forest,
watching an emerald painted door
slowly drying in the moonlight.

There's a strange silence, and I'm
waiting for the day to dip
over fields of endless rapeseed.

With no place to go, no place to be,
I catch a piece of paper flying in the air
and ask it what will happen next.

What happened next in the dream (II)

A white silhouetted man like a faceless tailor's dummy flipped from standing to upside down foretelling an oddness that would become ordinary. While a new normality took its first breath, yesterday suddenly became a different galaxy. Yet I remained in the eye of misfortune, viewing things with my feet in the air, my head on the ground. Picking at the frayed rug, I started to look at things differently; I began to appreciate the melody in my attic. Dear Psyche, you prepared me somehow. Your message in dream, last Harvest Moon, was a gift. I had time to ponder the dream while I tended to the ivy in our garden. Six months later, and two hours after our first lockdown kiss, I finally understood. My higher power had passed me a message about humanity, a magnified glass held above a world of pavement ants and their shadows. All that was left was a blank white page or else a white mannequin waiting to emerge from our closets, and a wondering about what will happen in this afterlife. Time is liquid wax. I no longer remember my dreams or else recall the mundane. I wonder if this is a sign that everything in this world has in fact now vanished. I've wasted my nights. Now my body hears everything I don't see.

I look back upon the before, think beyond what I cannot see.

In The Hypnotist's Chair

Straight lines may look perfect on paper
yet deep in the folds
of *sleep*,
we find fault lines.

With one ear
open to the script of your life,
you observe jars of peaches,
pickled eyes,

lining the childhood pantry
of your timeline.
We regress before speech,
beyond thought

while the chair's frame
creaks – and you lick your lips,
I try your words in my mouth
    and time hops,

lumbering from one age
to the next
in trance.
You enter back

with a craving for tinned fruit
and we both notice a dying bee
orbiting the brown light
in the middle of the room.

Far-away footsteps intercept;
and we shake hands.
As you leave you fasten a parachute
to your father's back,
        and he free-falls from the ledge.

Shadow Integration

I am waiting	little nightmare
this time	I am watchful
beyond dusk	fragmented
in sleep	restless
before we meet	a visit
to a hotel bathroom	spinning
while my feet	skim the ceiling
of sleep	to boundaries
in a soundless	cellar
in dream	I wake lost
behind wild lupins	recalling
my plan	to call for you
shadow, now	I chant
and you rise	from a house fire
guarded	by ancestors
arms placed	around your fury

we fuse into white night, hands untied
left with a sense of the way life tugs
and a fistful of coal sealing the hollow

Form borrowed from Emily Berry.

The Cake Mixture

After Edip Cansever's *The Table.*

a woman creams butter
and sugar in a mixing bowl
one, two, three yolks

and a tiny piece of shell
she adds the coldness
of milk and evening air

echoes of mothers
calling their children
the darkness in the room

she places in the bowl
conversations from her body
muffled like folded egg whites

loud edges of dreams
a French nursery rhyme
she makes a well and places

marbles from her mind
her shadow
counting each precious breath

she peers at the purple sky
drops an eclipse in the batter
the cake mixture puffs

sighs just a little
then a deafening calm
yet the woman keeps adding things.

Golden Shadow

When you are lonely in the darkness of night,
Diving into rain clouds with chalk in your eyes,
If only you knew your astonishing light.

While the wind seems to know when all is not right,
In your head there's a jackdaw telling you lies
When you are lonely in the darkness of night.

Like the acorn in awe of oak's noble height,
You can't weather hope only yearn to be wise.
If only you knew your astonishing light.

You even burn silk, talk the sun into fight.
Shadow, why are you too brilliant a prize
When you are lonely in the darkness of night?

You cling to an envy of lotus in white,
Step out of the magic you try to disguise.
If only you knew your astonishing light.

When you feel happy spinning fast in flight,
I wish I could show you the dazzling skies.
When you are lonely in the darkness of night,
If only you knew your astonishing light.

After Persian poet Hafez: "I wish I could show you when you are lonely or in darkness the astonishing light of your own being."

A Moon's Love

For Evelyn Pema

I've prepared for my parting from this earth,
little Pema, by placing my love on the moon.
I thought I should write with detail of this,
just in case you can't find it under the bed.
The moon is now the keeper of all my love.
It felt like the obvious place to put it,
just as the moon sends its light to earth
the moon is also holding the love I have for you,
that way you can't miss it,
and seeing the moon can remind you of that.
I sometimes worried you'd leave it at home,
so I've asked the moon to keep it for you,
you can also ask the stars for some,
I've left a supply with them too,
the way I'd put extra tissues in your satchel.
When you look at the moon and stars
you can be reminded of how I love you,
beyond the limitations of photographs, fabrics,
my memorial stone or mala beads.
When I am no longer in the world
you'll find my love when you look at the moon.
You won't forget that will you, my Lotus?

Italicised text from His Holiness Gyalwang Karmapa, Ogyen Trinley Dorje,
the 17th Karmapa, head of the Karma Kagyu in Tibetan Buddhism.

Hypnopompic

I will think upon the night in the openness of space
a place to recall wild dreams, dying and mantras
whisper away hardness and loss, slip beyond
soft blankets and beyond words
as I rest in unborn hopes
deep in alpha

deep in alpha
as I rest in unborn hopes
soft blankets, and beyond words
whisper away hardness and loss, slip beyond
a place to recall wild dreams, dying and mantras
I will think upon the night in the openness of space

The Fertile Void

beyond each encounter
   after every complete   turn of cog   close of life event
    after your last   sip of   morning tea   what happens?

in the silver-grey   land   between your planet's moon
   and the sound   of your last yawn
there's a terrain   half-forgotten   a place of leg-room

before your next crusade

after the rise of thirst   and the sweet quench of water
   do you   soak up   satisfaction
     or swiftly   hustle towards the next?

   at the end of a car journey   before you ferry on
       what would it be like   to turn off the engine
and notice how it feels   to land?

in this hot-waiting-room of   not-much-happening
you may anticipate a strange   sensation coaxing you
   why not   float on your back   weightless

  at the end of a love affair   instead of starting   a new hunt
notice what emerges   listen to your own   drum beat
although it may be tempting   to pluck dangling opals

   touch the silk violets,   what if there's more that lies in the
        sphere   of *unborn awareness*

after a day of digging   and pruning
on a spring afternoon   instead of hurrying indoors
what would it be like to   sink your bare heels   into the dirt

soak up the rawness   become part of the ground
    if you notice restlessness   unearthing you
   don't be disheartened   remember   you are cobalt sky

if you feel the tug of busy   ask   what grows
in the   space   after   there may be moments
   of enlightenment   incandescent light-licks

when you dwell in this unknown   hanging out
   with only the here and   now   you may find peace
    you may find nothing
                    rise
you may find your next happening   like a natural
phenomenon,   from a richer   spontaneous
place   of meant to be

you can't stay in the void forever   but it's good to stop by
before being led to your next orbit
   until then   enjoy defying gravity   in a figureless place

embrace   the interval between the end
and your next sensation   you might not always
        see   it's raining diamonds

Indigo Dreams Publishing Ltd
24, Forest Houses
Cookworthy Moor
Halwill
Beaworthy
Devon
EX21 5UU
www.indigodreamspublishing.com